Brief Encounters with My Third Eye

Selected Short Poems 1975-2016

Bruce Boston

Crystal Lake Publishing
www.CrystallakePub.com

Copyright © 2016 Crystal Lake Publishing
Be sure to sign up for our newsletter and receive
a free eBook: http://eepurl.com/xfuKP

All Rights Reserved

First Edition 2016
ISBN: 978-1-68418-758-4

Interior illustrations by
Luke Spooner

Proofread by
Paula Limbaugh, Sue Jackson, and Joshua L. Hood

This is a work of fiction. Names, characters, businesses, places, events and incidents are either the products of the authors' imagination or used in a fictitious manner. Any resemblance to actual persons, living or dead, or actual events is purely coincidental.

No part of this publication may be reproduced, stored in a retrieval system, or transmitted in any form or by any means, without the prior permission in writing of the publisher, nor be otherwise circulated in any form of binding or cover than that in which it is published and without a similar condition including this condition being imposed on the subsequent purchaser.

Poems in this collection first appeared, sometimes in slightly different form, in the following periodicals, anthologies, and previous collections by the author: *Aboriginal SF, Abyss and Apex, Aeon Speculative Fiction, Aliens and Lovers, Amazing Stories, Aoife's Kiss, Asimov's SF Magazine, Balticon Program Book, Berkeley Poets Cooperative, City Miner, Conditions of Sentient Life, Dark Regions, Dreams and Nightmares, End of an Aeon, Fantastique Unfettered, The Freeman, Full Unit Hookup, Fungi, Hardware, Interstellar Navigation, Jack-O'-Spec, The Literary Hatchet, Lone Star Stories, The Magazine of Speculative Poetry, Mythic Delirium, New Blood, New Myths, The Nightmare Collection, Night Cry, Night Songs, Outposts of Beyond, The Pedestal Magazine, Poetry Quarterly, Poly: New Speculative Writing, Resonance Dark and Light, Science Fiction Age, Semiotext(e) SF, SFPA Poetry Contest Winners 2014, Silver Blade, The SPWAO Showcase, Speculative Science Fiction, The Stars as Seen from this Particular Angle of Night, Star*Line, Strange Horizons, Surrealities, Talebones, Tunnel Road, Velocities, Weird Tales, Z Miscellaneous.*

Contents

1970s

- 1   Artist as Owl
- 11   The Alchemist Is Born...
- 12   Night Flight
- 12   The Beast at Vespers
- 13   Horses of Light
- 14   Soul of a Victorian

1980s

- 17   The Alchemist Discovers a Universal Solvent
- 18   The Alchemist Takes a Lover...
- 19   A Word Before the Ice Wars
- 21   Ouroboros
- 22   Ancient Catch
- 23   Of Time and the Sidereal Shore
- 24   Denizens
- 25   The FTL Addict Fixes
- 26   For Spacers Snarled in the Hair of Comets
- 27   The Berserker Enters a Plea...
- 28   The Evolution of the Death Murals
- 29   The Knowledge at Londrai
- 30   All of the Lady in Sly Concoction
- 31   Beyond the Edge of Alien Desire
- 32   The Mating of the Storm Birds
- 33   Clear to Eternity
- 34   Dead Heat
- 35   Curse of the Demon's Wife
- 36   A Hero of the Spican Conflict
- 38   In the Eyes of the Pilot

39 The Nightmare Collector
40 Against the Ebon Rush of Night
42 Cruse of the Werewolf's Wife
44 Mean Time Tomorrow
45 The Sizing of Curses
46 America Comes
48 Old Robots Are the Worst
49 The Inevitability of Light

1990s
53 Curse of the Shapeshifter's Wife
54 Curse of the Angel's Wife
55 A Spacer's Life Is Ice and Fire
56 Born a Royal Beast
58 Rara Avis
59 Curse of the Time-Traveler's Wife
60 Curse of the Body-Thief's Wife
61 Future Present: A Lesson in Expectation
62 Stars May Rise to Hell and Back
62 Curse of the SF-Writer's Wife
64 Interior Monologue with Mirror
65 To Dine with Poetry and Mathematics
66 California Noir
67 Gravity Drives the Blood
68 In a Palace of Stone
69 The Veracity of Imagination
70 My Wife Returns as She Would Have It
71 New Colors and Old
73 The Evening News on the Morning After…
74 Conditions of Sentient Life

75 Curse of the Ghost's Wife
77 Curse of the Bandersnatch's Wife
78 Spacer's Compass
79 The Poetry of Science Fiction

2000s
85 I Build Engines
86 The Man Who Lives in the Attic
87 Freakish Confirmation
88 Surreal Domestic
89 Of Glass, of Fire, of Elements Abundantly Defined
91 Robovamp
92 Shells: The Next Generation
94 Why Your Robot Dog Has Been Recalcitrant
95 The Filing Cabinets of K.
96 The City and the Stars
97 Dali's Ego on Karloff's Frankenstein
98 Revealing Their Eyes
99 Origami Rockets
100 Tale of the Bluegone Boy
101 Heavy Weather
102 Shadow Light
102 Ghost People
104 Knife People
105 The Slums of Atlantis
106 The Dimensional Rush of Relative Primes
108 Visions of the Blue Clone
109 Cat People
110 No Need
111 Conflicted as a Warrior Poet

113 Dystopian Dusk
114 Gargoyle People
116 The Last Alchemist

2010s
121 A Life in the Day of
122 Lizards and Wind
123 Surreal Wish List
124 Middletown, USA, 1953
126 Relative Weights and Measures
126 The Lateral Eclipse of Bound Sunsets
128 Noir People
129 The Music of Particle Physics
130 Tourists from the Future
131 When Beyond the Furious Clouds
132 She Walks in Yellow to Please Her Lord
134 Containment
134 Surreal Couple
135 Intimations of a Dead Immortality
137 Septuagenarian Flashback
138 Slicing Time
139 Surreal Shopping List
139 Here
140 The Music of the Stars

142 Award Poems in this Collection
143 Acknowledgments
143 Omissions
144 Contributor Notes

1970s

Artist as Owl

Do I feel
an affinity with owls
because I watch everything,

or because
my feathers are so soft?

**The Alchemist Is Born
in a Sudden Changing of Seasons**

Each winter morning,
bare and heavy,
apprenticed to the fires
of the smithy's shop,
he bore his trade upon his back,
he forged his soul to cooling metals.

Plangently the hammer would ring
in the day's first stillness,
loud against a chalky sun,
sending the wrens to higher perches
in the oaks and sycamores,
the deserted reaches of the barn.

Such blows would shake his teeth,
drop sparks about his ankles
and singe the hair
upon his turning arms.
Each falling arc trembled
the air in its breaking.

One day he watched the sun
drift north, bright as his furnace.
The snow had fled the gables,
and by the morning roadside,
soft crucibles of gold
opened among the leaves.

Climbing to the loft
he was stunned, left speechless.
There in the darkness,
pale as old straw,
the pulsing throat
of a bird he could not name.

Night Flight

Boots wet, you return to the tower.
You shake your hair from the scarf.
Come close beneath the covers.
All the clocks are melting.
I will search your back for wings.

The Beast at Vespers
after Jean Cocteau

The daisies turn blue at dusk.

The moon is the rib of Adam,
and the night,
a woman grown around it.

The carcass of a fawn
bloodies the garden path.

Horses of Light

As the storm runs west at dusk
the light gives up the air,
the lurching sea turns dark
and sleek as otter skin,
a great bloody horse blooms
in the sun's red setting.

Dali has penned such rearing cumuli
in moments of rare attraction,
the flecks of mica on the table
shining beneath his ringed hand,
the waiter with a single absinthe,
the sun always down to dark waters.

Prophets and mariners can mount
these blood and cloudy steeds.
They gather the sky's loose reins
to ride against the night
with long hair streaming,
feet lodged in stirrups of air.

In the wake of avid hooves
the sky lies sleek and dark,
the plumping stars mere flecks of stone.
While other hands are ringed by sleep
the waiter brings a tray of drinks,
heady absinthe, seagreen pernod.

Soul of a Victorian

Too late, you have signed the deed,
when you hear a wailing in the cellar.
You find her blind and stubborn
as a root, naked, draped in old lace.

As you lift her through the trapdoor
the wind begins to pierce the eaves,
to fill the high and narrow rooms
with the reek of wood's damp rot.

She tells of the graves in the yard:
one cat, three dogs, a fetus.
She speaks of an empty carriage,
the rusty stain on the hall paper.

And while you are listening
you taste the dead hours and grasp
the worms' artless consummation:
you feel time between your fingers.

She is slipping back from you,
down to the dark lampshades,
the chest with the broken hasp,
to photographs of forgotten memory.

1980s

The Alchemist Discovers a Universal Solvent

When the moment
nicks my consciousness
keen as a dagger's edge,

fast as the laws allow,
more silent than
the elasticity of bone,

I cross the continuum
and stand beside myself
with senses flaming

and body turned to stone.
For one fractured instant
sand hangs in the glass,

the breath of the forest
catches in its limbs,
a slice of the natural

and relative universe
is stretched on the block
with light suspended:

a still life taut
on the lip of a dream,
until the moment turns

and thought is upended.
The forest shakes itself
and time reassumes

its interminable ticking,

the steady dissolution
of all it subsumes.

The Alchemist Takes a Lover in the Infinite Variety of Fire

In the arcane wilderness
far from the commerce and rage
the artifex and his soror mystica
watch the precious distillates
stream against the glass.

Male soul and female spirit
they seek not only the alcahest,
the *aurum vulgi* of the day,
but night's subterranean coin,
an *aurum philosophicum*

of sure golden illumination
cracked from the celestial egg.
Sulfur and quicksilver fuse
in the depths of their study,
a sleeping deity stirs

in the bellows of their breath:
the sick metals are cured,
a glowing stone revealed.
Far from cities and nations
in the untamed birdsong wood,

the alchemist and his lover
join bodies and minds

in rites of transmutation
to feel their warmth ascend.
From calcination to sublimation

in the *vas hermitca* of self,
mercurial essence is renewed
by flight dazzling and precise.
Fire, as it leaps against the grate,
never dances the same dance twice.

A Word Before the Ice Wars

From the high towers of Riva
you can already see
the white walls of death to the north.
They catch the winter light
and return it to the sky
in colors strangely bright,
as if fires burned
upon those icy slopes.

Each storm is worse,
each day our lands grow smaller.
Entire villages now lie lost
beneath the frozen mass.
Outlanders of every description
crowd the streets of the capital.
The palace walls are scarred
and the king waits alone,
wrapped in his bed of furs,
with no solace but a fiery brandy

to burn the chill from his soul.

Our neighbors to the south
have closed their borders:
no passage, no trade.
The wineskins run dry.
I hear the clank of swords
rising from the courtyard below
as men prepare for a war
not of their choosing.

Some say we should not have
left the gods of our fathers,
and to appease their ancient rage
sacrifices have been taken,
fresh blood for the old altars.
Some say a sorcerer of the North,
a malicious polar wizard,
has placed this snowy curse upon us.
Others shrug and look to fate.

Indifferent to such speculations
the great cold cliffs
continue their descent.
The northern sky is a fury
of light and icy color.
One can almost hear
their implacable growth
grinding down upon us like waves,
the breakers of a frozen sea.

Ouroboros

Long torso lashing,
dark water streaming,
I rise from the sea,
my scaled sides a flexed
and living geometry
upon the night.

Poison glistening in
the facets of my tongue,
stars flecking my hide,
I fly against the moon;
my tail, the antidote,
slithers behind.

I slough off death,
raise the bodies entombed,
reap the bone orchard,
clothe these ivory sticks
in fast failing flesh
to reap them once again.

In the restless bondage
of my sleek embrace
I encircle the earth
like a devouring lover.
I consume empires
and cough up history.

I eat dead souls and
feed each wanting womb.
In the curve of my coils

the wailing faces
stretch and tighten.
Endlessly, I swallow.

Ancient Catch

The fisher casts his lines
when morning is only
an attenuation
in the wet smoke
that wreathes the water
thick as tule fog.

On steppes above the sea
where shadows run,
and even shadows
fall thinner
than shadows once fell,
deserted cities are
baked in red clay.

Cities sway perceptibly
in the rush of centuries.
The fisher's catch lies
writhing at his feet:
sleek and monstrous,
goggle-eyed,
more atavistic than the
broken skulls at Olduvai.

Hunkered and shadowless
in his bank of fog,

the fisher tends his lines,
nurses a bruised hand,
from the crease of
a knuckle licks the patterning
blood: warm and saline,
on this lip of land,
above a shallow sea.

Of Time and the Sidereal Shore

Time and again
I have known the moment
that is ever spawned
in the onrushing change
of dark to dawn

and down again.
I have seen it light
upon the breakers
and dash against the sky.
I have watched it curl

along the dunes,
elongate and limpid,
slippery as a skin of oil.
As petals flare
against the foliage

and the sea cliffs
rise about me,
tier upon staggered tier
studded with greenery,

a vertical prairie

of succulents
living from the rock itself,
how the seconds tremble,
how the light
runs to slaughter

in the swerve and bend
of gravity's calling,
how the star-streaked waves
contain the night
and all of space beyond.

Denizens

The wired saints
have chosen their saints' day
to march forth
from their wired citadel
and move among us.

Along the slanty streets,
down crooked hills,
past empty boulevards
and darkened shops,
their procession thunders:

clanking on metal legs,
wearing suits of light
pure and invulnerable,
one a great slab of ocean,

fish darting in its depth.

A few lone citizens
trapped upon walkways,
pressed back against pillars,
watch with paled eyes
as the throng lumbers past.

And we watch from our windows
as the tread of their
heavy grace shakes the city,
these gods of our making
who now move among us.

The FTL Addict Fixes

Beyond the system's fall,
upon a hill in empty space,
my mind recalls
in spokes upon the sky
the glint of colors newly named.

My mind recalls
the taste of patterns raw,
of bone and blood
and matted thought as one.

In pale resolution
cabin walls shimmer and flee,
and I am nailed free
to the struts of a flailing universe,
specked to each bald star.

A being and nothingness
on the tense of time.

Come faster sweet steel,
give me your light sinews,
your latticed and crystalline flower,
the abstract particulars of your death speed.

For Spacers Snarled in the Hair of Comets

If you've heard the stellar *vox humana*
the untuned ear takes for static,

if you've kissed the burning eyelids
of god and seized upon the moon's

reflection, disjointed and backwards,
in the choppy ink of some alien sea,

then you know how sleek and fleshy,
how treacherous, the stars can become.

While the universe falls with no boundary,
you and I sit in a cafe of a port city

on a planet whose name we've forgotten:
the vacuum is behind us and before us,

the spiced ale is cool and hallucinogenic.
Already the candle sparkles in our plates.

**The Berserker Enters a Plea
on the Death of Greater Los Angeles:
Not Guilty by Reason of Insanity**

I was just another could-be maniac
like any other plebe,
living from drug to drug,
hopping strato-jets,
bending out for a week on uppers,
catching the heavy holos
whenever I could,
awaiting the click of inspiration.

I was just another hightech madman
in a long suit and flatcap,
ticked by tension,
teasing the deadly dials,
spacing in the chain cafes,
visioning the latent disaster
in sixteen dollar lasers
and backpack megatons.

I was only another serial lunatic
about to go it all at once,
jump riding the endless strips
from cordon to cordon,
squinting in the carbon sunlight,
imaging random slaughter:
flash frames of red devastation
on the flesh crowded streets.

The Evolution of the Death Murals

Flash shadows remain on the walls
and pavements of the ruined cities:
silhouettes of detailed accuracy
with arms outstretched and heads
thrown back, line the empty blocks
or lie upon the streets' decay,
elongated by the angle of the blast,
yet clear as forms that were human.

Such tableaus are "death murals"
to the old survivors, who shun them,
who mutter and turn their eyes away.

Those who were children in the times
now past, have fulfilled the metaphor
these words convey: they've fleshed
and suited the figures with paint,
with scraps of cloth and papier-mâché,
so here and there a few stand forth,
instantaneous terror upon display.

They've taken anonymity from clay,
and in the faces have portrayed
the annihilation on its way.

For the children with no knowledge
of that world, the dismembered city
is a labyrinth they roam at will:
the artifacts are incomprehensible,
and the figures poised in mute array
have become nothing more than targets

for the barbs of splintered metal
they now fashion for their play.

The Knowledge at Londrai

Earthen souls or souls of star flight,
the same demons with hides of fire,
the same angels with nebulae wings,
prance upon each of our chests,
dance to all of our songs
as they are piped and blown
past the bellows of our breath
and recede through the worldly ages,
faithfully structured on the facets
of the crystallized dwarf stars
housed in the library at Londrai.

Honeycombed in the ultimate alloy,
a series of temporal half hitches
in the stubborn fabric of existence,
against the bellying singularity
that claims our universe en masse,
we discover nothing has changed:

Still we play and learn our way
through corridors and coups d'état,
past forests and spiked metropoli
we continue to sail the dying seas
in crafts of gold and glistening foil
propelled by thought alone,
and yes, we never cease to sing

and dance as the darkness and light,
the shifting dipoles of the ever life,
evolve to a common extinction.

Through immense star caverns
that enclose our prison of space,
we know at last the knots will slip
and the unstoppered seconds rage.
We know the walls will ravel and crack
and the maw-beast will appear,
swallowing planets and stars
in its jaws of billowing black.

Beyond the stochastic horizon
where breath is but a cage of fire
beneath the brilliance and the horror,
and the crystals of Londrai have imploded
on the splintered cusps of space-time,
we have seen our doubles dancing
in the nascent star stuff of our graves.

All of the Lady in Sly Concoction

Once the initials of the kingdom
are carved in bittersweet dalliance,
the Queen eats only fleurs-de-lis,
continuous abalone of a suave persuasion,
an occasional valence of mass hysteria.

Often we have heard her lemming
in the raw corn silk of the night
-- argumentative Gatling, endless

whalebones, meretricious knees --
all of the lady in sly concoction,
irreparable as the bare velocity
of her bodice-torn meat.

And this we know and this we are,
camouflaged and flogged by sleep,
as if the rain that seeps along
the flowering crevices
and streaked crenellations
of Cyclopean warriors, proud
to serve Her Majesty's exposed
exaltations, could actually feed
the dark and mouthless children
who defile the square.

Beyond the Edge of Alien Desire

Seduced by pheromones
more potent to the senses
then my species' own,
I ride her blue cries
to crimson excitations,
and for a trembling instant
the light years between
our limbs collapse.

Charged by the tendrils
of her spiked electric fur
to telepathic sight,
I feel pain raining down,

see blue fields blown
in the searing light,
know the wiles of victims
for the pale glabrous beasts
who handle them by night.

At dawn the dreadnaughts leap,
another world to take,
her scent is still upon me,
blue miles to go before I wake.

The Mating of the Storm Birds

When the storm birds cry and rise,
their great wingspans
white against the violet day,
or dark upon the stars,
we know the wind and rain
lie soon behind.

Safe within our metal hulls
for weeks at a time
we hear their fierce ecstatic
krees! as they ride the gusts,
their song a descant
within the storm's dense pounding.

Afterward it is silent
but for the drip and pool of water.
The red sun returns to the violet sky,
and here and there across the muddied landscape
we find them: feathers smudged,

huge beaks slack, bones twisted
like the struts of broken gliders.
Their eyes, close on the moment of death,
still shine with a luminous intensity.

Across the valley in the nesting cliffs
fledglings hop awkwardly
up and down the dark escarpments.
They will wait through a year
of slowly changing seasons
for their own moments
of grace and joyous expiration.

Clear to Eternity

There is no mercurial soul in the duplication
of consciousness, no will to life or death
in the nuclear powered automaton of me.

The mind uprooted from its failing flesh
drifts through limpid seas of logic and ennui,
over patterned chips where the finest details

of personal history, the moments of triumph
and the moments of shame, have been recorded
faithfully, yet stripped of all emotive force.

I cannot smell the fire or the bread; the sea
I cannot feel; this damp salt breeze that
filled me once with thoughts of wanderlust,

I register on sculptured metal cheeks,

I see now only as the precursor to rust.
In the wait states that replace sleep,

yet resemble a clear and porous reverie,
I can no longer don the vestment of dreams:
I am imprisoned by digital immortality.

Dead Heat

In a summer midnight of bourbon
and bougainvillea, of bones in heat,
the pheromones of the dead rise up
and their bodies rise in turn,
a sweet nausea of putrefaction,
a corruption from beyond the grave.

Past the copse of cottonwood
where failed flesh is coffined,
the moon pierces these shades
of passion unspent in life.
A ghostly concupiscence is released.
See how they dance like spurned angels,
dionysian with madness and relief.

Senseless as the damp black grass
or the rotting jasmine leaves,
their desiccated torsos clack
and clack in frightful copulation
as they swallow their own grief.
Their ghoulish voices undulate
and siren through the streets.

While beyond the bougainvillea
and the sweating windowpanes,
beneath some spired gothic ruin
you down another glistening drink.
You wait with leaded glass in hand.
The clock's shaped like a cicada
and it's far too hot for sleep.

Curse of the Demon's Wife

She dreads the scaly amours
of his infernal touch more
than his eternal indifference.
Each time he returns home

from his nefarious calling,
he calls her to their bed
and elaborates upon life
and skullduggery in the

world above, he complains
of Lucifer himself and
the partisan politics of
the netherworld, of how

he has been passed over
again and then he raises
one huge and horny palm
against the flesh of her

side, and she starts to
quiver in what he mistakes

for passion, so he slowly
sates his own in rounds

and conjurings of perverse
imagination, her long nails
splintering on his glossy
impenetrable hide, cries

rising in the dank forest
where their mansion stands,
where the nocturnal trees
bloom on for centuries,

where their long departed
children, no longer demons,
no longer fiendish and sad,
are faces in the branches.

A Hero of the Spican Conflict

I'm talking blood, mate,
when the lasers come on target
and there's scrap flying everywhere,
when human skin shreds like paper
and the red keeps raining down.

I'm talking heat, brother,
all at once and plenty of it,
when the probes find their mark
and those rooted and toothy carnivores
that pass for trees begin to moan.

Heat enough to fry your eyeballs
and high broil your brains,
unless you're head deep in a hole
you've hacked for yourself from
the bleached and bone hard soil
of this extraterrestrial hell.

I'm talking plague, man,
alien viruses fragging your genes,
pustules sprouting on your forearms,
and when the ampoules are gone
you kill your company one by one
and still the sickness rages.

I'm talking pain and desolation
and the damn damp jungle closing
down around you like a sleeve,
until you're the last one,
alone for a night of two days
in a world full of unclassed toxins,
the darkness rife with monstrosities,
an acid rain burning your breath
and etching scars upon you cheeks.

And each time they send you up
salvaged and rebuilt for combat,
the stench of death grows heavier
in your mind until it's palpable
as your own artificial flesh,
until whatever remains of the you
you once knew is less and less
use to them or you or anyone.

I'm talking pensioned, friend,
pastured and propped in the sun,
restructured to the finest details,
a mind full of unrelenting horror,
the table full of medals before me,
a metal chest to pin them on.

In the Eyes of the Pilot

The breath of many worlds
sifting through her blood,
a wealth of alien images
overflowing the faceted orbs
of her mind's projection,
she shapes unlikely geometries
of spatial condensation
and leaps unerringly
on the template of the stars.

Here she is alone in the dark
and stretched very thin,
four thousand tons of steel
and flesh trailing behind,
patterned and at one
with the universal birth
of stellar excitation.

Here the Doppler fractions,
and each line of thought
that clicks smoothly
in the breach of acceleration,

instantly threads
the shifting parameters
of force and inclination.

Always the light returns
like a relentless assassin,
the attenuated atoms assemble
and she unclips the sensors
to breathe again: her thought
once more is only thought,
her eyes, blue cognizance
fixed in transient space,
reflect her destination.

The Nightmare Collector

Each night he calls you
for the leading role
in his gallery
of ancestral tableaus
that trails back
through the Pleistocene
to the red primeval.

From the endless slashes
in his voluminous greatcoat
you can feel the heat
of captured bodies
invade your rumpled bed
with delirium and fever,
you can smell a brassy

sediment of tears.

From the hollow blackness
of his flapping sleeves
you can hear the pulse
and thump of unborn shadows,
a dense hysteric fugue
winding up and down
the bones of your sleep.

The nightmare collector
waits on the landing
in the unlit hall
where the instruments
of ablation are arranged
on cold leather pallets,
where the dreamer's
balustrade of terror
rushes across landscapes
of a darkening retina,
where snakes coil about
your arms and ankles
and draw you down
bodily into a forest
of bloodstained hair.

Against the Ebon Rush of Night

Our near immortal historians,
who lived the eons they describe,
now clothe the past not in events,

mere stitches in the warp of space,
but in waves and pulses of racial death
and racial consciousness formed again,
not in systems that rise and fail,
but in each species' finite travail,
the generations of life force spent
against the ebon rush of night.

Our near visionary prophets,
illuminati all to the fifth degree,
have foreseen the oncoming expiration
of our species' evolutionary seed,
and warned the present of future wars
and someday kings and alien dreams
that will transpire before our eyes,
they've cast tomorrow on fallen skies
and traced our waning soul's descent
against the ebon rush of night.

Our near omniscient scientists,
grave as truth in their gilded labs,
recombine the elemental strands
of genetic lace to fuse our cells
with breath, our veins with fire,
to give the lie to cosmic fate
our polyclones are cloned again,
we fashion selfscapes without end
where light can flare and break
against the ebon rush of night.

In the far realms of sovereign space
where stars and worlds begin to thin,

and the darkness of intergalactic
wastes begins to dominate the mind,
the technosavages storm our gates,
barbarians who share their flesh,
artless creatures fiercely bred
who plunder parsecs as they spread,
exultant with their swift ascent
against the ebon rush of night.

Curse of the Werewolf's Wife

By the time the moon
is replete and brimming
and his transformation
is complete, she has
prepared herself accordingly
with liner and with shadow,
a touch of rouge upon each cheek,
the barest gown to accentuate
her vulnerability beneath.

This time she spends
before her mirrors is used
to bait his awful needs,
to sate his raging appetite
and hold him safe within
her arms while others
of his fated breed
are driven forth by hunger
to roam the night town streets.

Each time the madness
in his eyes is captured
by her artistry, she endures
a dreadful ritual of rape,
she tastes his lupine breath,
she knows that now familiar
scent so animal and sweet,
the heavy musk that fills
the air to saturate her dreams.

By the time they awaken
he will be a man once more,
who remembers not a moment
of his brief and brutish spree,
who will glance in stray amazement
at the bruises on her flesh,
the blood upon the sheets,
as he begs her for forgiveness
in a voice that makes her weep.

But time will prove her enemy
in spite of all he's said,
the constant cycles of the moon
will turn upon her once again,
and when her slender limbs
have begun to lose their grace,
and when her beauty flees,
what spell will tame this beast
who nightly shares her bed?

Mean Time Tomorrow

As the styles run from ostrich to beaver,
from sleek and unadorned to recherché,
from white to basic black to chromatic,
as the names across the marquees ripple

in a rain of hours and the language
evolves from vital through decadent
and disappears in a polyglot rush,
as this civilization or that shudders

onward in post-coital convolutions,
mean time was never half so mean,
cracking away like a metronome whip,
filling our veins and arteries with

fast compulsions and ascensions
while we hammer out totalities
to cerebrate the changing race,
cause mean time was never so mean,

mean time was never half so flash,
past Greenwich and beyond it crackles,
trailing away like a metronome scream,
past Arabian wells and American towers,

tracking the sky with eclectic cameras
that define both eventide and dawn,
while straight along the noon highway
where the sun splinters on manic chrome,

where the engines are aligned seriatim,
the road signs lurid as commandments,

the pavement glazed in acidic light,
the drivers all ratcheted and stoked,

we can see the sellers and the users
stepping up their motions once again,
cause mean time was never so mean,
mean time was never half so flash,

unrelenting as the pull of history,
miniaturized on photonic faces,
elemental as the bestial pedigree
in an all night factory of mutation.

The Sizing of Curses

Small curses are the swiftest.
Anonymous and hard to track
as rats within the walls.
Invisible until they bite
and maim the child in its crib,
then fade like bloody smoke.

Middling curses are more perilous,
more apt to betray their maker.
One false move and the shadows
can turn like dogs upon a master.
Yet fiercer they are than dogs
and faster to the throat.

Master curses are for the adept.
You must learn the arcane writ
by heart and renounce all thought

at the level of dark illumination.
You may then slay your enemies abed
and scorch their lands with light.

Curses all are cursed again.
The ones they are wrought upon
bear the edge of their harsh magic.
For ones who forge such flinty spells,
the weight of their casting
hangs and hangs within the head.

America Comes

america comes
in tortured lunchrooms
with tiffany palaver
with the hard yellow yolks

of strangulated gumshoes
america comes
in commercial breaks
sweet tocsins on the tongue

a filth of spavined dogs
imported from the hague
in small copper buckets
america comes

with subcutaneous lunges
soft bullets
and hard caresses
a plinth of technosavagery

billeting her breastbone
far too much
not nearly enough
these are the tongs

the assassin breathes
into his blood
as the distended winter
continues to arrive

enamored with
its own body cast
full of greasy assignation
far too much

not nearly enough
the assassin winces
at his own replication
as he flesh tastes

the bitter meat
of metal on his chest
america comes
at the base of a ravine

where a nest of beetles
who have eaten
one another's legs
roil like jumping beans

where an old car mirror
with a rusted socket

reflects the spoils
of ejaculation

Old Robots Are the Worst

Lurching down the stairs,
asking questions twice,
pacing in lopsided circles
as they speculate aloud
on the cycles of man,
the transpiration of tragedy,
debating the industrial revolution
and its ultimate unraveling
in sonorous undertones.

And all the while
they are talking and pacing
and avoiding our calls,
we must wait and listen,
annoyed, yet with increasing
wonder at the depth and breadth
of their encyclopedic knowledge,
the strained eclectic range
of their misunderstandings.

And all the while
their tedious palaver grows
more sophistic and abstruse,
the nictitating shutters
of their eyes send and receive
signals we have yet to translate,

a cyberglyph of a language
composed of tics and winks
and lightning exclamations.

At last they come to answer,
to wheel us to the elevators,
and you know, despite their
incompetence and intransigence,
beyond their endless babbling,
one gets attached to the old things,
inured to their clank and shuffle,
accustomed to the slow caress
of their crinkled rubber flesh.

The Inevitability of Light

To keep the night
from curling up at dawn
they built a nail
the size of a mountain,
an entire gross of nails
and a hammer like a moon.

They drove those nails
along the horizon,
deep into the earth's crust,
deeper still in the mantle.

The night stretched,
stars jumped and blurred.
They heard invisible pinions
wrenched from their sockets

and a tremendous tearing
as slashes of cerulean
sheared the darkness
and shadowy ribbons
trailed across the land.

And since that day,
the beast of night
has had a ragged tail.

1990s

Curse of the Shapeshifter's Wife

He transforms himself to a long-dead relative
to scare the wits from her visiting mother

and send her packing. He slithers beneath
the locked bathroom door like Plastic Man

to take her dripping wet in the middle
of a shower, and although she must close

her eyes from the horror of his chameleon
incarnations, his instant appendages explore

all the fine nooks and crevices of her body
with such prehensile precision that she can

not fend him off until the water turns cold
and she is polymorphously pleasure-spent.

Just for the fun of it he becomes a chandelier,
a checkerboard Dalmatian, a bearded potentate

with a bejeweled satin turban and escargot eyes.
Each time she is angered by his endless antics

she finds herself confronting a giant teddy bear,
so darling her arms ache to cuddle him forever.

And when she summons the courage to betray him,
at the moment of a momentous climax, a momentary

respite from his ever altering round of alterations,
he reveals himself as the very stranger in her bed.

Curse of the Angel's Wife

The milk silken embrace
of his six-foot wingspan
drapes her in a coverlet
of staid domestic desire.
The loose feathers she must
vacuum on a daily basis

drive her up the wall.
He is perfect to be sure.
Just like their marriage.
Just like their lives.
A spacious townhouse
in an affluent suburb

of the Celestial City.
Two and a half children.
Summer vacations in Jamaica.
Thanksgiving with her parents
in Denver or his in Rochester.
Christmas at God's doorstep
with the Hallelujah Chorus.

Only there are no Roman candles.
No dicey dives into the ink blue
waters of some icy Adriatic
while the stars shine on.
What should be the limitless

reaches of Heaven have become
for her a precise Purgatory.
And as she moves incessantly

from one color-coordinated room
to the next, upstairs and down,
she knows it will always be such.

Always she will welcome him home.
Always she will be a mother of two,
pregnant with this barely half a child.
"Hallelujah!" they will shout and they
will sing until their lungs are bursting.
Loose feathers blowing everywhere.

A Spacer's Life Is Ice and Fire

Inward along the speckled arm
of our turning spiral nebula
I FTL-ed it in whatever ship
would gain me ready passage,
so raw and green at first
until the burning darkness
laced my spacer's boots.

Inward through parsecs
of always changing light
and chill blue slumber,
awakening on worlds
where sense or passion
claimed my heady flight,
yet only in the passing.
So very green at first
until the rush of night
claimed my spacer's soul.

Inward to the epicenter
of our churning star swarm
where thoughts ineffable
could flourish and bloom,
where the universal light
at the galactic core
could fuse my sight
with visions quintessential,
with rich illuminations
beyond what's understood.

Burning green to metagreen,
a rush of colors in between.
Mandalic moons, sidereal seas.
A spacer's life is ice and fire,
graced by iridescent dreams.

Born a Royal Beast

Born a beast
in a bestial land of discontent
I made no covenant with dreams,
no compromise with pale priests
who worshiped blind divinity,
unsheathed my blade at every chance
to cleave the flesh, to crack the bones
of any man who barred my path,
and kept my castle dark and mean,
its dungeon deep to house the screams.

Raised a beast

by a bestial man of harsh intent
I gave no quarter, asked for none,
no woman tamed my raging need,
the wenches sighed within my bed,
young virgins bled upon my sheets,
I rode the hunt into the dawn
upon a steed of vengeance black
and slew my father heedlessly
to claim his thorny crown of greed.

Praised as beast
by bestial men of hellish bent,
I took no pleasure in such things,
no friends to share my shadow plight,
but the falcon call and the battle din
filled my days and spent my nights,
I scourged the land with devilish deeds,
and those who preached of sin to me
soon tasted steel on their tongues
and spoke no more of any king.

A dying beast
in bestial shame who could repent,
I've left no living kin to mourn,
no grieving wife to wail and weep,
with the stench of age upon my breath
my earthbound flesh awaits its last,
I hear the throngs within the street,
the pale priests intone their cant,
I curse their mumbling litanies
and dream of angels while I sleep.

Rara Avis

While the pale unicorn
hides in the faerie wood,
you fly for the sun
in gold and crimson raiment
to solo the empty sky.

While the fearsome griffin
devours the thief,
while the winged dragon
swallows its tail,
you dine on valerian
and cinnamon.

While the fetid breath
of the scaly basilisk
withers shrubs
and splits rocks asunder,
you fashion a nest
for your own cremation.

Of all the magical beasts,
only you, sly phoenix,
can glide the shadow
lands of death
and fish the River Styx.

Only you, mad bird,
go down in fiery plumage
to rise again
from the sizzling marrow
of your bones.

Curse of the Time-Traveler's Wife

No telling when he'll drop by for
a spot of tea, a change of history,
a bit of the old slap and tickle.

No telling how many of him will.
Now he has folded his life so often
his mind is creased as an accordion,

so whenever his multiple personas
-- youth to man to nonagenarian,
callow, arrogant, sage -- congregate

for their dry-heated conversations
of Möbius trips and Klein hostels,
temporal loops and fractal revisions,

she endures an endless bickering,
a devil's-advocating one another
up and down the carpet until

she feels the lines of her own life
are entrapped in the circuitous
ambulations of an Escher print.

Give me a solid man, she thinks,
some victim of foolish consistency.
Not this simmering kettle of fish

diced with yesterday's doggie bag
and next Sunday's standing rib.
Not this will-o'-the wisp who

contradicts his own contradictions,

who worries the bird from its nest,
never hatching a lasting decision.

Curse of the Body-Thief's Wife

When he inhabits another man's soul
and rides another man's life
he becomes an amalgam
of self and other,
a hodgepodge of desires and needs.

When he inhabits a woman's soul
and commandeers another life
he becomes an amalgam
of self and other,
a hodgepodge of warring sexes.

When he straggles home to her,
shedding skins and hatching schemes,
forever on the mend,
hoary long before his time,
he turns uncaring eyes
on a world he's left behind.
He's lived far too many lives
for a man of petty dreams.

When she impales him
on the ivory warmth of her embrace,
bodies stretched upon the bed
in double crucifixion,
her beauty and her grace

are like a stain upon his scowl,
her innocence in need of devastation.

Future Present: A Lesson in Expectation

The future the past once envisioned is
nothing like the present we now inhabit.
No aerocars. No globed and spired metropoli.
No eccentric rube-goldbergian gadgets that
deliver a cool drink and a shiatsu massage
with the casual flick of a single switch.
No passage to the stars or even Mars.

And what of those gently purring walkways
lightly peopled by superior beings who glow
with the logic of a sublime moral grace?

Instead the present through which we slog
and stagger seems raw and tatterdemalion
as the past we expected to trash behind
--the current is the cruelest century--
breeding sex plagues out of ignorance,
rife with demagogues and despoliation.

And while we ponder what roads not taken
have abandoned us to this frantic moment,
this vain dyspepsia of the modern mind
--no one answer, a gross on every side--
the tomorrow we envision is omnivorous:
mushrooming clouds, displacing populations,
devouring civilization with toxic fungal rains.

As those purring walkways recede and fade
into the dimming distance of the mind's eye,
the future, second by ever-rivering second,
oblivious to all expectation, yanks us bodily
into the coagulating rapids of its own design.

Stars May Rise to Hell and Back
for Mitch Snyder

Clouds are gray at Stinson Beach.
Gray gulls give up their cries.
And hunger has no mouth to sing
beneath the pale of lowering skies.

And hunger has no mouth to sing,
no thought, no voice for sorrow.
Wind is hard at Stinson Beach,
cold again as cold tomorrow.

Waves can break a rock to shore
and never mean a bloody thing.
Stars may rise to hell and back,
and hunger has no mouth to sing.

Curse of the SF-Writer's Wife

Sandbags. Anchors. Lead weights.
Sacks of grain. She's tried every
kind of ballast she can think of.

Hemp. Leather. Silk. Chain link

Steel cable. Every kind of leash
and collar she can possibly fashion.

Yet every time she turns her back
he takes flight with his imagination
once again and is off to the moons

of Jupiter or the red sands of Mars.
The uncut lawn continues to grow.
The garage continues to clutter.

Oblivious to such domestic concerns
he resides within his own creations.
Where's Daddy? the children screech.

He's working, she always tells them,
never really believing it herself.
If only it paid the bills more often

she might buy it as a "kind" of work.
But she knows play when she sees it,
selfish play of the most trivial sort.

In her darkest moments she prays
that the far distant future will
accelerate on a lightning course

and rush to meet them overnight,
that somehow in the flip of a switch
science fiction will be science fact,

that all the possible fancies he might
invent will already have transpired.
Maybe then he'll find an honest trade.

Interior Monologue with Mirror

The cartographer who dwells behind my eyes,
who maps the continents of desire and imagination
for the navigator who charts the course of dreams
and nightmares for the pilot who traverses
the landscapes of time and illusion where
fabulous cities come and grow and go,
inhabited by creatures human and not so,
whose tales resemble those living and dead
as forecast by mages and twice-told by poets
on foolscap and parchment in volumes still read,
that relate and regale the sentence called life
and all it entails -- the passing of passion,
the hero's hard quest, the war on the mountain
waged for a woman, the bittersweet warmth
of the sun falling west -- while I watch from
a distance and wait in a queue, and turn
out my pockets and rummage my baggage
in search of a ticket for lands I once knew,
and wonder which flight holds my name
written full, what map's jagged passage
shows which way to go -- are the engines
still revving? does the jet stream still flow?
should I drink from the fire and dance
in the snow? could I lose/find my self
in the quickening reflection of some
high afterglow? -- I blink for a moment
and toss back my head -- the water
is running, the steam fogs the glass,
I see that the blood on my razor is red.

To Dine with Poetry and Mathematics

The mathematics of poetry
is irregular in the extreme,
an unbounded system
approaching absolutes
the way parallel lines
converge at infinity,

an incomplete accumulation
always in the act
of redefining itself,
or some other act
equally outrageous,
as inconsistent

and sure as the sea.
The poetry of mathematics
is clean of line and form
with all elements in place,
like a bullet clicking
into an oiled chamber,

like the finely calibrated
path of the rocket's glide:
graceful equations flow
with absolute and enviable
precision to a vanishing point
where all questions are null,

all balance is defined.
When poetry and mathematics
sit down for dinner

the evening is vintage,
the conversation moves
by leaps and starts,

like time or evolution,
like the human imagination
as it tunnels and jump cuts
from occlusion to conclusion,
from a well of mired thought
to the heights of light sublime.

California Noir
after Ross Macdonald

In dingy sunset motels
scattered along the Pacific Coast
dead bodies surface
with horrid regularity.

Unsolved homicides one and all,
who are these corpses
but card-carrying members
of some lost American dream?

Stabbed, shot, strangled,
bludgeoned senseless
by the proverbial blunt instrument,
sprawled across mattresses,

on cold bathroom tiles,
spread-eagled and face down
in kidney-shaped pools,

their bloated features
mock our ingenuity.

Noir as the night,
indifferent as the stucco or sand,
they offer no salty sermons
for the unwary.

Crying sirens taunt us.
All our hardboiled figments
jackknife into the breakers
of an oil slick sea.

Gravity Drives the Blood

Past sunlit fountains where scattered
rainbow droplets fall to its calling,
over the graceful arch of the bridge
that reflects and defies its calling,
in the roaring whoosh and swoop
of wild carnival rides of wonder
that leave us breathless in the air,
gravity bends the light and drives
the blood that courses in our veins:
when we reach up it calls us down,
keeps us spinning round the sun,
defines the span of night and day.

In words that fall from our lips,
in the river run of images that
rush and flow through our brains,
always tumbling into the past

in the moment of their calling,
gravity drives the blood and bends
the light that courses in our veins:
it shapes the stars, breaks our bones,
spills the clouds onto the ground,
sets the boundaries of our play.

From the wail of birth's hard fall
to the coffin's silent roped descent,
from the pull of an age that was
wide and weightless to the weight
of miles passed and years defined,
gravity bends the light and drives
the blood that courses in our veins:
it breaks our bones, calls us down,
keeps us spinning round the sun,
fuses cells and time and flesh
and takes our breath away.

In a Palace of Stone

She sits all alone in a palace of stone
on a planet that circles a dying red sun.

Unlike her sad sisters who soon became crones,
whose bodies are dust and a shovel of bones,

she fashions her youth from a series of clones
who feed in the darkness until they are done.

Her suitors are fiends who seek only to own
--not her life, not her flesh, not her soul--

but the secret she holds in a bastion of stone
that keeps age at bay while the centuries run.

Friends are long dead, her name is unknown,
her world is a barren one all sane men shun.

Her beauty's a sin that she cannot atone,
her days are far empty, her passions undone.

She sits all alone in a palace of stone
like an unchanging sculpture of obsidian.

Chilled to the bone, she feels the sky moan,
as she waits for the death of the sun.

The Veracity of Imagination

Impossible...they once said!
Nothing moves faster than light.
It's beyond the constraints
of the space/time continuum.
Yet now we do it every day!
Blood and sweat and calculation

sends these behemoths flickering
through the interstellar dark
to emerge beside a farther star.
Human desperation/aspiration
to transcend the static moment,
to deliver any given reality

our FTL-minds can comprehend:

this is the force that drives
our being through the night
and folds the fabric of space.
And as the planes of the plenum
open to us, one way or a dozen,

open like the palm of a hand,
like a wound, like the wings
of the gigantic lepidopteron
of Fretas IV as it first senses
the rays of its blue-white sun,
the unconstrained universe

will be splayed and revealed.
Impossible...they always say,
as they have learned to say.
Meet me in shades of tomorrow!
And remember, we are forever
touching the body of space.

My Wife Returns as She Would Have It
for Maureen

"I'd come back as a butterfly,"
she often told me, "a Monarch
or something equally as beautiful."

Eleven days after her death it happens.
I am walking a block from our house
when a quick flutter of velvet wings,
dark against the pale dome of the sky,
passes left to right inches from my face,

causing me to pull up short in mid-stride.

Turning to the right I see a butterfly
has landed on the sidewalk at my feet.
Black and brown shadings striated by
vermilion bands, speckled with white.
(Not a Monarch but a Red Admiral,
I later discover in one of her books.)

"Is that you, sweetheart?" I whisper.
I am a fifty-six-year-old man suddenly
kneeling on the cement spilling out
his love and regrets to a lone insect
he hopes is a reincarnation of his wife.

Clearly as beautiful as any Monarch,
an epiphany of color in my flat world,
the butterfly appears to be listening.
Brilliantly hued wings shift slowly
up and down as if they sense the
coarse human sounds filling the air.

Even once language deserts me,
it/she remains a moment by my side
(together like partners after a dance!)
before soaring into a sky all-at-once blue,
vanishing into her future and my past,
alive and free as our finest memories.

New Colors and Old

Pomegranate blue. Stormsilk. Raw orchidine.

Auraviolet sun blur through the xellor trees.
A windy opalescence plashing shadow play
with the olvre cumuli of an orangedown sky.
Dark-light dappling the untouched landscape,
the metacolored flora and surrealistic fauna
of this brilliantly hued otherworldly world.

If your thoughts could frame a shelter
for the tossing trees, if your heart could
preserve the unique life forms that abound,
if you could nourish these wilds untamed,
you might christen every color -- plumbaro,
szale, levantura -- and savor every shade,
you might discover passions equally unnamed.

Soon others will pass through the xellor trees,
others by the hundred and the hundred score,
sporting colors ordinary and long overused,
born and bred on some other starflung world.
They will come in a ragged unending array,
trampling the spectra of painterly scenes,
invading these wilds with undeclared war.

They will see your land with leaden eyes,
sun and shadow a stage for their strife,
lay claim to the forest and all it contains,
with unrefined passion and everyday lies.
"Colors?" they'll say, raising their palms,
shading their eyes to censor each sight,
squinting to block out the glorious light,
"Only for children and artists and fools!
Abandon your madness and join us in life."

**The Evening News on the Morning
after the Final Solution**

Lean as a severed head,
mad as a midnight runner
with hot blood upon
his face and hands,
the sentences scroll
past fort-mansions
and warrens of the dead,
past luminous cadavers
and martial bands
on slaughter parade.

In a back moment,
after the leaping
and the grinning,
after the sell songs
of corporate crusades,
the rendered hours
heel and lockstep
in a flicker-sham
of genteel articulation.

So who what when where
how are we to listen
with a knowing care
to the raw scansion
and bald jabber
of pixel-thin lips
that smile through
plague and devastation,

of teeth that flash
the box scores
of genocidal rage,
of tongues so slick
with carnage they can
call the darkness "day?"

Conditions of Sentient Life

The human condition
does not vary that much
from one system to the next,
from white suns to yellow
or red...nor does the alien
condition for that matter.

Sustenance and procreation,
Play and work and slumber.
The soothing balm of dreams.
A share of nightmare terror.
The brilliant riot spectrum
of speculative imagination
in all its shades and scope.

We are no more than animals
who have learned to assemble
and dissemble volatile hearts,
our stories and lies and creeds,
to create worlds internecine
as the storms that rail within,
to transpose the static patter

of our own nattering souls
to the multiverse at large.

Birthed in blood and tears
we often go down the same --
alien arthropod, human biped,
unexpected creatures of flesh
and shell and contradiction,
of breath and its expiration,
cellular chains and molecular
clusters in constant evolution,
recycled from the stuff of stars.

Curse of the Ghost's Wife

To spend the day
sated and insecure,
never knowing where
he stands or when
he could appear
with strange demands
from beyond the veil.

To hear the creaking
boards and realize
her lover's tread
is no different from
the witless sighs
of her haunted house
settling into ruin.

To wait through

the darkening hours
for his milky white
ambulation to solidify
and beckon her to bed,
where he rides her long,
with no mean effort,
into the chiaroscuro
of incipient dawn.

To see him rise up
from their excitation
and try on shapelessness
as shadows take,
to watch him stream
beneath the door
like lathered smoke,
to feel his ectoplasm
dry in strange ineradicable
patterns on her sheets,
to sense the silence
of his ever presence
closing down about her
like a graven sleeve,
to spend the day
sated and insecure,
to wait through
the darkening hours
for his milky white
ambulation to appear.

Curse of the Bandersnatch's Wife
with apologies to Lewis Carroll

She gired mimsy youth with him
and others of his frumious ilk,
like Brillig and the slithy toves,
the ill-beholden Prince of Silk.

Despite the joys of frabjous love,
and uffish evenings spent in thrall,
she can't be sure where Bander is,
nor even when he'll come to call!

On tulgey nights the Jabberwock
runs chortling in the forest prime,
galumphing past the sith and sledge
beneath a moon of blevous lime.

One, two. One, two. Sleep has fled
-- whenever Jabber burbles nigh!
She counts the gimbled stars by pairs,
outgrabes her reach of beamish sky.

She jubs the gate, lums the lights,
alone with vorpal sword she waits.
With eyes aflame, jaws that crack,
the Jabberwock calloohs her fate.

And so a manxome life she leads,
gloomed in asperants and bleers.
Even Bander's snick-snack songs
can never reliquate her tears!

She gired mimsy youth with him

and others of his frumious kind,
like Brillig and the slithy toves,
the ill-bespoken Prince of Wine.

Spacer's Compass

South I shipped...galactic south
    spanning the reaches of unbounded space
      through the moss stars and beyond
  hanging with this crew or that
      a rough lot they were
      or some just strange
  stranger than you'd care to know
    for a light year or two on the fly

West I wandered...galactic west
      leaving lovers changing friends
    past clusters hanging in the heavens
      like burning ingots and bands of flame
  landing always in a different land
    a ready cup for alien ways
      seeking never so much an answer
  as a fix...a frame of reference
      to sift my strangeness from

East I flew...galactic east
  against the words of wiser souls
    to decaying grandeurs steeped in fog
      and cultures deadly spent
    to language worlds and pleasure worlds
  and the mother world or fabled so

      a desolation of rust and snow
         heir only to its past

Old I grow...galactic old
  the polar night now calls my name
    and still I tramp the stellar routes
      from burning white to burning red
        jump cutting lives and lands
     fixing no frame of reference
       beyond the passage itself
         adrift in the passages
          yet to be taken

  Space has no directions
    and holds all directions at once
      a well of radiant possibilities
    all matter of strangeness

      ...and the stars are for the living

The Poetry of Science Fiction*

Against the fall of night,
across the wounded galaxies,
envoy to new worlds,
behold the man –he, she, and it!–
born into light, dying of the light,
becoming alien between worlds,
a new species more than human
always coming home
alone against tomorrow.

Time and again, those who can,
change the sky and all between.
We cast down the stars,
four hundred billion stars
on wings of song.
Brightness falls from the air,
downward to the Earth,
down the bright way
burning with a vision.
Earth abides, a swiftly tilting
planet in the ocean of night.

Explorers of the infinite,
exiled from Earth,
dancing at the edge of the world,
we call back yesterday
in memory yet green.
We return to Earth
but we are not of the Earth.
The future took us out there
across the sea of suns
in search of forever,
beyond the blue event horizon
where time winds blow.

Lest darkness fall
you shall know them.
Strange relations. Strange
ports of call. Strange horizons
from utopia to nightmare.
Star-line velocities ten thousand

light years from home.
Men like gods. Women of wonder
holding your eight hands.
The shape of things to come.

The stars are ours -- take back plenty!
Dream the creation of tomorrow!
Dream the last dangerous visions!

Except for changes in punctuation and capitalization, this poem is composed entirely and verbatim from the titles of science fiction books and periodicals.

2000S

I Build Engines

I build engines
from the lines of battle
no matter how they are drawn.

I build engines
from the lungs of drowned sailors,
their last breaths billowing the waves.

I build engines so lubricious and lubricated
you can feel them in your blood
before you hear them.

I build engines that churn entire continents
without revealing a word.

I build engines that feast on copses
of burning hair and thickets of eyelashes.

I build engines from milk and meat
and the decanted semen of aborted generations.

I build engines as natural as the habitats
they immure and incinerate.

I build engines from the babble lust
of court whores and camp jesters,
the confessions of the desecrated and shamed.

I build engines from the sins of the fathers
and the rumored indiscretions
of mothers and wives.

I build engines that fill your boots

with scorpions while you sleep.

I build engines that jackknife your dreams
with ingenuous apparitions
and ingenious doppelgangers.

I build engines from ivory and scrimshaw
and the jawbones of apes.

I build engines
from the lines of battle
no matter how they are drawn.

The Man Who Lives in the Attic

Her best winter coat and gloves.
A rare figurine, Henry Moore copy,
limited edition, Zurich, 1943.

A bottle of sedatives. Her CD
of Joachim Zane. All of this
and more missing in the last week.

She finds the bread left on the
counter, open and stale. Empty
jars and cans in the garbage.

The fridge has been rearranged
and the milk keeps disappearing
though no glasses are dirty.

She imagines him standing in
the dark kitchen. Drinking from

the carton. One arm resting on

the open refrigerator door while
the light from within spills
across his jeans and bare feet.

She sees him roaming the house
in her absence, reading her
letters, touching her clothes.

She suspects that sooner or
later she will have to do
something about him. But the

days have been short this year,
her dreams rich and satisfying,
and he may not be real after all.

Freakish Confirmation

At the age of fifty-five
I receive substantive evidence
for what I have known
since I have known
anything at all.

After X-raying my spine
my chiropractor blinks,
and blinks again.
"You have two extra ribs!"
she tells me. "And one
extra sacral vertebra!"

I am a freak of nature.
A mutant under the skin.
A skeletal overachiever.
That one in a million
and a half kind of guy.

Back on the street
I open my chest,
remove two long bones,
toss them into the clouds.
"Make me a couple women?"
I say. "Eve-like and tempting?"

The extra vertebra
I decide to keep for awhile.
At least until I figure out
how sacral it really is.

Surreal Domestic

I open the refrigerator and instead of food
it is stocked with automatic weapons
and hand guns and ammunition.

I make love to my wife and find
that she has a third eye
where her navel should be.

I have a clock that makes a different noise every hour.
Sometimes it sings like a bird.
Sometimes it is a train pulling into a station.
At least once a day it is a bullfight or a shuttle launch.

I took it to a jewelers to have it fixed.
He told me not to fool with it or it would melt.

I have a giant flea for a pet.
It has little dogs running around on it.

When I turn on the TV the stereo comes on.
When I turn on the stereo the toaster heats up.
When I pop a slice of split-topped wheat into the toaster
the garbage disposal begins devouring itself.
I have all of this memorized.
It changes every day.

At the back of my walk-in bedroom closet
there is a giant zipper that runs
vertically from the floor to nearly the ceiling.
I have never touched it.
Believe me.

Of Glass, of Fire, of Elements Abundantly Defined

When the Empire of Glass,
the Kingdom of Stone,
and the Interregnum of Fire
sat down to tea in Harlot Woods
it was a time for great rejoicing
to the ends of the fogbound world
where dragons swim free.

Never had such paradoxical
and inbred dignitaries
(deities?) (dogmas?) (dialecticians!)

confronted one another
in a setting of spatial import.

"This t-t-tea is c-c-c-cold,"
screamed the Empire of Glass.
"My rolls aren't p-p-pouffed!"
Breaking into a thousand shards
and reforming again with
each stuttering line.

The Kingdom of Stone was silent.
He took a swallow from his flask
and with one granite protrusion
swept cups, saucers, silver,
and candelabra from the cloth.

The Interregnum of Fire scoffed
at the two horrible images
who dwelt by his sides.
He burned hot, he burned cold,
as was his wont he twinkled
mightily and he burnt
Harlot Woods to the ground.

This is how the day can
unravel in strict confusion,
with ceremonious cartwheels
and unmasked conflagrations,
all along the Periodic Table
of Elements abundantly defined.

Robovamp

Blonde and beveled,
lithe and pneumatic,
the clichéd image
of a teenage boy's
rough libido at play,
she stalks the dark city
in chains and in leather,
in high lace-up boots
to gather her eager prey.

Her titanium skeleton
is sheathed in faux flesh.
Her face is a mask
carved from a dream.
Her pulse and her breath,
and the light that resides
in her teal-shadowed eyes,
are both less and more
than they seem.

Given most men
are sixteen-year-olds
at the unfulfilled heart
of their sexual plight,
her suitors are legion,
they queue in long lines,
they shiver and sigh
and throw back their heads,
to savor her sharp overbite.

As she drains their life force
to power her own,
to fuel her fine form
and feed her stark mind,
she never asks why
some return to her side
and are willing to die,
addicted to fright,
tranced by her final caress.

Though she often wonders
as dawn stains the sky
and the sun cuts the night
with its fiery blood-red crest,
just why her creator,
the one who designed her,
who built and refined her,
was her very first victim,
willing as all the rest.

Shells: The Next Generation

There are no shells on the beach.
The children have taken them all.

Watch them come and go at lightning speed.
See them explode running from vans, RVs,

cars of every description, school buses
proclaiming public or private origins

in block letters on gauche yellow sides.

Screaming children whose banshee clamor

startles the flight of wheeling gulls
into broken circles and torn ellipses.

Small children whose eyes glitter with
the greed of their chance acquisitions

and whose mouths are often pursed in
an arrogant and self-serving assurance

of their own supremacy in the universe.
The adults in their charge follow slowly,

incapable of damping the vicious avidity
of their progeny or of prying bright booty

from the clasp of sharp and tiny fists,
their distended bodies collapse and sink

by infinitesimal degrees into the sand.
Overcome by the heat and a lethargy

induced by their constant procreation,
they survive for the next generation.

At dusk a lone beachcomber wanders
the trampled and deserted shoreline,

a sloppy hat upon his weathered brow.
His shell collection is far from complete

and there is no hope of completing it now.
He unearths merely a few shattered remnants,

notable only for how their grained interiors

can sometimes shine with muted intensity

in the swiftly failing horizontal light.
Tomorrow he vows to rise at first dawn,

to begin his trek before the onslaught,
to claim rare finds fresh from the brine.

But in truth he is a family man himself,
long beleaguered by children of his own.

There will be no time for singular pursuits
before the day and its shells are gone.

Why Your Robot Dog Has Been Recalcitrant

You feed him too many nuts and bolts,
not enough rivets.

You scolded him for killing the Doberman
who lived next door.

You ignore him most of the time
and then expect mutual joyous affection
at the oddest most inopportune moments.

He has read far too much Sartre.

You can't find the instruction booklet and
the lights blinking suddenly and insistently
on his chest mean nothing to you whatsoever.

He's never been the same since he lost
his tail in the mower.

He's been talking with the robot cat.

The Filing Cabinets of K.

One hundred and sixty channels
yet little that speaks to
the presence of being alive
and its complications
in the 21st Century.

On the radio or the Net
much of the same nonsense,
news and cant of the day
recycled for the next generation
in a slicker and sexier style
more likely to entertain.

Assuming that death
in its shabby threads
with a charm for the children
can entertain and entrance
the always eager hordes.

Assuming the threads
mass produced for all of us,
defined by fashion mavens,
can cover the gravest sins
from birth to the grave.

Somewhere in the last drawer
of a battered old bureau,

or jammed to the back shelf
of an abandoned closet,
a consummate document
of the age lies waiting.

Perhaps not a document
but a collage or video.
There may be thousands
of such hidden creations:
welded junk sculptures,
rock sonatas, oil paintings,
etudes for instruments
yet to be refined.

Even the most dauntless
and incisive expression
can mildew and rot forever
in the filing cabinets of K.

Even the cleverest dogs
cannot cross the bridge
facing an endless stream
of unrelenting traffic.

The City and the Stars

The city is there regardless,
enormous in its conceit,
hard as the stare of a beggar,
sharp as a skyscraper's teeth.

The city is full of power.

Claim it with credit or cash.
Electrons racing to midnight.
Engines igniting the past.

The city is always laughing
at those it harbors and shuns.
The city is rich as a bakery,
thin as a trail of blood.

The city is small as an insect,
immense as the life it contains,
adrift in space like a beacon,
devoured by time and decay.

The city is very terrestrial,
dark and light as it comes.
Stars are strictly for backdrop,
eclipsed by the neon suns.

Dali's Ego on Karloff's Frankenstein

A fragile brute
to be sure.
Full of angels and rage.
Delectable in his frailty.

I would build him differently.
Extend his limbs across
monolithic landscapes,
launch great protuberances
from his neck or torso.

Give him a crutch or two
to keep him upright
in his willful indecisions.

I would grant him color
and drench him in absolute
until his countenance
was sad boiling.

I would make an image
more beautiful and horrible
than any scientist
mad or otherwise
could ever envision.

For I am Dali. The artist.
Striking the cymbals
of long imagination.

Revealing Their Eyes

Dali never
looked to the starry night
like Van Gogh.

Van Gogh never
looked to the secret life
like Dali.

Yet the layers
of paint
on their canvases

reveal sunflower
burning giraffe
eyes.

Origami Rockets

They float to the moon
in origami rockets.
Astronauts from

a childhood fantasy.
The moon smells
like a green apple.

They walk freely
on its skin without
helmets or spacesuits.

They build a town.
Stores and houses.
Schools and libraries.

A street fair with
lots of free parking.
And the moon people

come to live there.
Up from their craters
and their moon caves.

A gentle sleepy race.
Just the right sort
to carry our dreams.

Tale of the Bluegone Boy

The gravely hordes of Sweverton swept down to meet
    the Arbiters.
The Arbiters wore claws and wigs, a world replete with
    their own sun.

"Listen!" cried the Bluegone Boy, his eyes like agates
    blazing high,
"In the ruins and clines of Sweverton, dogs are barking
    as they run.

"And strafed along Van Glower Lane where peacocks
    break their stride,
the men and ladies, gentle both, have shored their
    specious pride.

"Listen hard!" he cried in pain, his voice blown
    cat gut wild,
"We can die in bed or die with spurs, but they'll
    never let us ride."

They put the Bluegone Boy in chains, strapped him
    tight to Swever Gate,
all through the bangs of dirty day and in the
    hollow point of night.

Beneath the bruised black clouds he hung until
    his tongue lolled dry.
The ravid hordes and their liken ilk knew Dread Time
    had arrived.

So we strive in meant-to-be while blood flowers
    dark and light,

and the chosen of the hemisphere consume their
   spacious rights.

So we dream in ought-to-be with the craft of
   midden lies.
The stench that dwells in Swever Square is nothing
   to our lives.

Heavy Weather

If gravity changed
like the weather,
covering the planet
in waves and pockets,

fronts and depressions,
there would be days
on which we could
not move an inch.

We would lie helpless,
strapped to the
slowly turning Earth
by a rain of weight

that limited both our
breath and movement.
We would have time
to consider the nature

of such an existence,
to daydream about

an end of the storm
and those perfect

feather days when we
could fly like birds
over cities and forests
as if we had wings.

Shadow Light
for Maggie

In the shadow of
the Magellanic Clouds,
where the stellar
dust sweeps gather

in their ornamental crafts,
beyond the flash of novas
as forecast by the Galactic
Bureau of Standards,

we will choose a world
to share and refine
with our eloquent
and bold imaginations.

Ghost People

If ghost people
were the world

we would roam

the empty highways
in search of life.
We would migrate

through the walls
of deserted homes
and become manifest

in abandoned bedrooms
and kitchens to briefly
touch the objects of

the real world in a
way less than human.
We would watch the

fine artifice of man
stealing into ruin
as the centuries

unraveled: highways
cracked to broken slabs
soon lost in wilderness,

cities collapsing stone
by stone into rubble.
We would learn to think

of the changing climate
we were unable to feel
not in months or years

but passing millennia.
We would track strange
species as they appeared

and flourished and evolved
to stranger incarnations.
We would see the earth

turn flat in its crumbling
and watch the seas recede.
With our memories intact

as the sun burned red,
we would howl louder
than the dying wind.

Knife People

If knife people
were the world,
we would all
be called "Mack."

It would be:
"Mack, slice this."
"Sever that, Mack!"
"Mack, did you make
this puncture?"

If knife people
were the world
it would be

full of holes
and torn curtains,
green harvests and
bloodied walls.

When you are sharp
you have to cut.

The Slums of Atlantis
after G. Sutton Breiding

The slums of Atlantis
are no different
from any other slums
(except they stand
in the perfect shadow
of harmony complete).

The dogs on the streets
of the slums of Atlantis
are no different
from any other dogs
(except their barks
have been stolen
for the heady dialogues
of Philosopher-Kings).

The waters that reach
the gutters of the streets
of the slums of Atlantis
are no different
from any other waters

(except they trickle down
from marble colonnades,
divinely sculpted statues,
and immaculate bas-reliefs
of a beauty supreme).

Those who live and die
in the ramshackle houses
that line the streets
of the slums of Atlantis
are no different
from any exploited breed
(except their necks are
cricked and their eyes are
hard and their thoughts are
mean from ever looking up
to a sublime utopian ideal
they will never achieve).

The Dimensional Rush of Relative Primes

When Theda slipped into
a life of leisure
on eleven planets,
she had no idea of
the alien opportunities
she would endure.

At the end of her
journey lay the instant
known as Earth.

Teeming as it was,
she remained human
among others as such.

She missed the sure
exaltations that stellar
realms had to offer,
the swift acceleration
and dimensional rush
of relative primes.

Most of all the slender
tripeds of Nine-Four-Three,
intimate in their bravura.

Someday she would teach
her children's children
about the wages of space,
how in traveling from
one world to another
you are transubstantiated.

In that telling she would
conjugate the rules
of her digression
and the subsequent
definition of a self
she could not deny.

Illuminating her past and
its brash indiscretions,
she would prove without

the sun of a doubt
that the stars are fire.

Visions of the Blue Clone

The first of her
came to me on the first night.
She was a woman of mystery
who sang the blues.

The second of her
came to me on the second night.
She had a history
like no other.

The third of her
came to me on the third night.
She was bright and cheery
and full with the fire
that makes life.

The fourth of her
came to me on the fourth night.
The fire was catastrophic.
The blue rains came down
and our wooden ark settled
on a rocky promontory.

The fifth of her
came to me on the fifth night.
We embraced as lovers,
like eagles in an aerie

far above the drenched desert.

The sixth of her
came to me on the sixth night.
We entered the star ways
and jaunted faster than light
to her blue sun.

On the seventh night
the six plus one of us rested,
lying between cool sheets
fashioned from the blue
universe of our flesh.

Cat People

If cat people
were the world
we would embrace
the sharp and furry.

We would slink
along the street
and dash across it.

If cat people
were the world
we would build walls
against the sea.

We would sleep
by day and wander

the haunts and heights
of our cities by night.

We would have flesh
delivered living
to the arena
of our choice.

We would delight
in our feasting
and celebrate
the deathful grace
in our play.

If cat people
were the world,
oh how we would purr!

No Need

No need to excavate the mine or the stream.

Gems and precious metals have been placed on the necks of chosen paramours.

No need to reap treasures of cradled civilizations or whittle the rot from gold.

Where relics reside they are wasted to clay in their own sedimentary dust.

No need to scale star registers or conquer icy peaks.

Imagination's wide leaps catch the passion of your

intermittent ascent and decay.

No need to document the record of your absinthe and antitheses in its rank array.

The boatman who poles the black river with his mutant dog has taken the measure of your lust.

No need to salvage trestles for a monumental image that will be maimed by survivors.

No need to conjure lizards from the mouths of quail.

No need to follow the mule's hard reins to enlightenment.

Wherein lie dream realizations already framed.

No need to hazard storms of memory and feel light crackle in your veins.

Time's shadow is a cloth you rub between your fingers to fix its texture and density in your brain.

No need to cast a legend from the toss of hair and bone.

Or exhume the stony corpse once it has been graven.

Conflicted as a Warrior Poet

Bold
as the teeth
of a werewolf.

Uncertain
as an intergalactic flight.

Sharp
as an email from
a corporate raider
on the rise.

Needy
as a hurricane survivor.

Hardened and hurt
as the injured victim
of an armed robbery.

Sensuous
as an imagined interlude
with a cinema icon.

Seething
as a moral condition
in the twenty-first century.

Inarguable
as the razor knives
and automatic weapons
of a survivalist.

Sweet and sickening
as the kill of an enemy
and its ironic complications.

Conflicted
as a warrior poet,

with blood on his hands
and songs in his veins.

Dystopian Dusk

If it had happened all at once
like a curtain falling swiftly
and blotting out the light,

if they had severed our choices
with the flash of a blade
both sudden and bright,

or leveled our lives
with some artillery shell's
whistling explosive flight,

if they had slapped blinders
on our eyes, narrowing our vision
to all they claimed was right,

we would have raised an alarm,
cried out in protest and
summoned the will to fight.

Yet each turn of the screw
that tightened the bonds on
our lives was ever so slight,

we barely noticed the
loss of our freedoms and
the limits on our sight.

Now we wait in the shadows
of a thickening dusk where
all cats are black or white,

and a bare reflection
of the sun's last rays
heralds a fascist night.

Gargoyle People

If gargoyle people
were the world,
standards of beauty
would be far different
than they are today.
The eye of the beholder
would adore the grotesque,
worship the malformed,
rejoice in the appalling.

We would stand still
for hours at a time
without flinching,
never blinking,
glaring into one
another's countenances,
baring our static rage
and indomitable horror
with pride for all
the world to see.

When shadows of the sun

or moon moved across
the lines and planes
of our chiseled faces,
umbra and penumbra
like shifting scars,
we would celebrate the
hideous chiaroscuro
that light and its
absence invoked.

The rains would darken
our expressions further,
mottling our features
like a pox, sending
the dirt from Heaven
coursing through our
orifices in torrents,
spewing from our mouths
and staining our lips
in muddied streams.

And when the winds
teased our cracks and
crevices and whistled
and thrummed through
the stone hollows
of our wrathful selves,
the music we would
make would be fierce,
lovely, rich, and mad.

The Last Alchemist

When the laws of physics
have nailed and sealed
the universe complete,
down to the last stray
molecule and rebel atom,
when even the quarks
Charm and Strange rise
to a balanced breakfast,
ontological questions
will become passé.

When the Unified Field
Theory is lucid fact,
not wistful speculation,
there will no longer
be the barest chance
of turning baser metals
to golden illumination,
and metaphysics will
be reduced to no more
than a bedtime game.

When the final truth has
been signed and delivered,
the last alchemist will
retreat to a birdsong wood
where green still thrives,
near a rushing stream
clean as a burning flame,
clear as a lover's glance

he has long since fathomed
in his deepest sublimations.

2010s

A Life in the Day Of

The majestic blooming
of the century plant
reveals petals of pure yellow
and stained cream,
distinct pistils and stamens.

I will love you, she said,
as Freud loved the id
in its trammeled fury.

The jaws of my brain,
adrift in opaque bestiality,
question the integrity
of a Pythagorean
reclining nude.

The heel stamp of my pen
assassinates the art
of nuclear mystics.

I will love you, she said,
as Darwin loved evolution.
Things change.

In an algid moment
the final consequences
of the abominable resonance
of a soft and hairy
architecture are revealed.

Diacritical exclamations!

The ravishing comprehension
of cannibal imperialism
by a paranoid critic.

I will eat you like the peach,
she said, I eat every Sunday
in the sky black morn.

Having teased
the sensitive mimosa
in the circular greenhouse
late that afternoon,
afterward,
he would drink peppermint tea
with the ghost of morning.

Lizards and Wind

The lizards were everywhere
and so was the wind.
There was no way you could
keep either of them out
that hard spring.

No matter how swiftly
you shut the door,
the lizards and the wind
would slip inside
that hard spring.

Darting over the floor
with inhuman speed,

they were far too fast
for a novice human
predator such as you.

The lizards were like
lemmings rushing
blindly over a cliff side:
there was no way
they could survive inside.

You would eventually
find their bodies,
dead and desiccated,
beneath a desk or armchair.

And once under the coverlet,
centered on your sheet
carefully as if a draftsman
had placed it there.

But the wind never died
that hard spring.

Surreal Wish List

A chalice with propellers.

The myriad cachinnations
of snow monkeys.

Reversible photo
of cosmic exploitation.

The grand piano
in the stone garden.

The Roman numeral
for zero.

An endless choice
of incendiary devices.

All the favorite passwords
of the illuminati.

Three clear bells
rung daily at eventide.

A chateau with blue eyes.

Middletown, USA, 1953

The fields are dry and spare,
the land more brown than green.
Spring is drifting into summer
without a breath of protest.
No rain. No promise in the sky.

Along Main in the hot afternoon
the old men sit in the shade
beneath sagging tarpaper roofs,
talking and drinking beer.

The kids drink soda pop,
riding up and down

the deserted street
on their bikes.

Some have clipped
playing cards
to the spokes
of their wheels.
The intermittent
rata-tat-tat echoes
off storefront windows.

Whenever a car passes
it honks at the kids,
and that echoes, too.

By dusk some old men
have to be helped home
by their sons or daughters,
or whoever takes the trouble.

Some may stay all night,
dreaming of the past and
a worthless promise of rain
beneath the star-scattered
bowl of the empty sky.

Throughout the city
the air is still as stone.
When a breeze stirs
it fades quickly
in its first breath,
as if the cook
at the local diner

has clamped
a lid on it.

Relative Weights and Measures

I'll trade you
a hundred pounds of feathers
for a pound of gold.

When I apply the yardstick
to the racing Bugatti
its wheelbase is shorter.

A quart and a half
of nepenthe drowns
seven drams of sorrow.

My unconscious mind
proves too large
for the ten gallon hat.

I'll trade you
three hundred pounds of butter
for a rack of AK-47s.

Whenever her hair
grows longer than her waist
she reaches for the scissors.

The Lateral Eclipse of Bound Sunsets

Never believing the awkward

scalpel of an invidious paraclete
or the razors of those recently
consigned to public scrutiny
could carve intaglios of flesh

deep in his paramour's arms,
how could he have imagined
the fleet collaborations and
juxtapositions of stained youth,
such a veritable inheritance

in the swelter of the moment
during a long dusk in Tours,
postprandial espresso and
hot buttered croissants
cooling on the marble table

of a crowded hotel balcony,
only a scattering of candles
and glowing cigarette ends
and unintelligible voices
to assault the shadows,

to light the closet of the sky,
while back at the atelier
you've rented for the summer
an impertinent Beaujolais
breathes a heady bouquet

of charcoal and roses
and unconsidered lives,
an inconsiderate choice
for an after dinner wine

when a beautiful mad poet,

a Rimbaud in his prime,
waits to whisper mystic
mythical verses in your ear,
while the inviolate legislature
rushes through high doors

of the burnished capitol,
demanding further restrictions
on the travel of holy spirits
and bound sunsets by the score
across international borders.

Noir People

If noir people were the world
we would forever roam
the crooked nighttime streets
and brutal alleys of a city
of shifting shadows,
our own shadows
rippling across sidewalks
and the dim facades
of deserted buildings,
swelling and shrinking
behind us and before us
as we moved from one
lamppost to the next.

If noir people were the world
color would abandon us

to be superseded by
a range of shadow shades
in subtle gray distinctions,
by stark chiaroscuro contrasts
invisible to a world of color.

We would live in cheap
hotels or tenement flats,
drink our liquor straight up,
tell world-weary jokes
and crack cynical smiles
from the sides of our mouths.

If noir people were the world
death could come swiftly
and without reprieve,
-- the fast flare of a bullet,
the moonlight flash
of a knife driven home --
and our blood spilled
upon the damp pavement
would be no more
than the color of night.

The Music of Particle Physics

is absolutely relative,
precise and differential,
linear and curved.

When you listen more
and more carefully

to its progressive
chord progressions

and calculated harmonics,
its convoluted waves
of sound grow more
particulate and fanciful,

with strange notes and
a stranger resonance,
like a room filled
with milling strangers

at a crowded party
you begin to wonder
whether or not you
should have attended,

where no one can find
the host or tell you
exactly what's in
the hors d'oeuvres.

Tourists from the Future
"If time travel is possible, where are the tourists from the future?" —Stephen Hawking, *A Brief History of Time*

Their incursions into our
world are invisible to us.

They have come and gone,
leaving no trace of their passage,

for each time they change our world
they change our memories in kind,

just as they change our lives.
We are novels or film scripts

in inconstant vision and revision
as each act or chapter transpires,

believing each stray moment
as real as our mercurial past.

When Beyond the Furious Clouds

When demagogues create the dawn,
when teeth are bared in ready grins
& our palms gloved by leather,
before the trucks begin to roll,
before the crowds' blood roar
& the crying in the streets,
before the word is broken,
the pennons muddied,
& the sky laved with fire…

Those were the days
of martial parades,
of legions & lexicons.
From each whorled fingerprint
we cast worlds of thought
taut as pennons on the wind.

Those were the nights

of spontaneous conspiracy
beneath the sheets,
of flight upon the bed,
our arms ready & linked
in the sun's first splinter.

Now the art of flight is lost,
arms toppled into the sea,
the populace become the rabble.
Now our prints are smudged
by a rain of ashes
& petals of madness flare.

When serried columns pass & pass
in ranks unending,
when violence scales the walls
& outside a dirty snow is falling,
flake after flake the same,
when beyond the furious clouds
we can no longer be sure
the heavens remain.

She Walks in Yellow to Please Her Lord
after Robert W. Chambers King-in-Yellow stories

She who serves her Lord
more than any rank courtesan
in His bloodstained seraglio.
She who severs the swollen
filaments of His deranged
desires over and again.

*She walks in yellow satin with
gold and bile and stark obituaries.*

She who wrenches love from
its appointed assignations
and calls down abominations
on its amputated miscreants.
She whose glittering eyes
once feasted on Antietam.

*She dines in yellow and savors
vintage decadence and decay.*

She who engineers the screams
of cherubim and retches on the
dreams of diminished artists.
She who expels streams of
insects, piss, and plastique.

*She seduces in yellow silk,
aroused by madness and death.*

She whose essence is embodied
in feverish yellow jungles
in parched yellow deserts,
in hydrocarbon sunsets,
in the cracked yellow soil of
bombsites and untended graves.

*She sleeps in yellow, her blond
mane thick on the pallid pillow.*

Containment

I lowered a box on the
machinery of the city.
It chewed its way out.

I threw a shawl over
a reflection of the sun.
It burnt it to a crisp.

I placed a frame around
the moon and it sailed
blithely past its borders.

I wound chains round
my strangest desire and
it wore them like ribbons.

I locked dissonance in
a cage like an animal and
it bent the bars and
escaped into the wilds.

I shoved Kafka, handcuffed,
into a patrol car and he
never stopped laughing
all through his trial.

Surreal Couple

They met on a concave plane
draped by lampreys.

When he had three legs
she had two mouths.

They lived in the quaint rafters
of a petrified basilisk.

He became an engineer of
delirious omelets.

She washed the anaconda daily.

He vowed to eviscerate
the anapestic gods.

Covered with invisible tattoos,
she had no time for latecomers.

All their children slithered
into the cruel garden and
returned as a beautiful disease.

Intimations of a Dead Immortality

In a world tamped down
to cimmerian shades,
streets and houses

thoroughly shrouded
by the shifting umbras
and penumbras of what

little light remains,
fields and forests
bound by darkness

beneath an indistinct
sky drained of color,
faint eidolons may

flicker across the
screen of your retina
with the herky-jerky

action of a silent film,
cast and crew dead,
trapped in repetitive

motion like the
forms that traipse
across your dreams,

testing the reality
of daylight wisdom,
stretching your mind

into the fearsome
realms of a senseless
half life that may

exist beyond death,
beckoning you to
join them in the

drear silence and
convulsive iteration
of their promenade.

Septuagenarian Flashback

Stumbling into the humid
jasmine-scented dark
from a midnight cinema
playing an iconic art film
rife with sidewalk cafes

and iconic actors whose
monochromatic silences
confabulated to a toxic
conundrum of pale angst
and lost existential loves,

my venerable thoughts
segue to foggy mornings
in a metropolis by the Bay,
wandering the slantwise
streets of stoned youth

and the fleeing tendrils
of a Guatemalan high,
a great golden bridge
aglow with the blurred
headlamps of early traffic

rising out of the mist,
glittering like some fabled
and fantastic behemoth
that could carry me to
a chameleon tomorrow.

Slicing Time

Take a photograph
and trap a slice
of time's instant
trapped in a rectangle.

Film a video and
capture a strand
of time's instants
from the past.

Speed up the video
to see an orchid
burst in full bloom
from its calyx
in only seconds,

or a monarch's
crumpled wings
burst in sudden
and startling color
from a drab cocoon.

Slow it down
to watch the sure
muscled grace
of a running
thoroughbred,

or the strange
range of expressions
that flow across

the shifting muscles
of a human face.

Surreal Shopping List

the autobiography of a trellis

a brisance of laughter
so loud trilobites pause to listen

noctilucent bridge mix (2 sacks)

a guerrilla theatre staged in ragged flesh

hallucinogenic cutlet with flies

ravishing inversion of sunflowers
stretching the skin of the eye

the burning bush

3 lbs Stonehenge

Here

We find our hero in the midst
of an azure dream of lust and

glory that will take him ten
years to eradicate from his

psyche until it portrays
a world so blank and turgid

it could birth any universe,
monstrous and miraculous.

After that every summer
doldrums was anticlimactic

as never-never childhood,
a brief residue of tears

lost in a lakeside village,
the maybes of the past

forming horseshoe clouds,
innuendo his last resort,

waiting for the maitre d'
and the immaculate check

in a leather folder engraved
with a history of tomorrow

on which he would place
his incarnadine stamp,

a message concise and wry
in his inimitable and often

totally unfamiliar hand,
scrawled by an innocent.

The Music of the Stars

The music of the stars is
so very faint it is drowned

by the sounds of the city,

the steady drone of traffic,
the whine of sirens wailing
through day and night,

the clamor of crowds and
the hubbub of the media.
The music of the stars is

so very faint it is lost
in the static of the rain,
the timbres of the wind

batting against the trees,
in the rhythm of waves
consuming the shore.

The music of the stars is
so very faint, yet there
remain those of a certain

mind and heart who listen
hard enough to hear it,
never completely sure

what kind of music it is,
yet convinced it is the
one they must dance to.

Award Poems in this Collection

Asimov's Readers Award

1989	Old Robots Are the Worst
1993	Curse of the Shapeshifter's Wife
1997	Curse of the SF Writer's Wife
2005	Heavy Weather
2007	The Dimensional Rush of Relative Primes

Rhysling Award for Speculative Poetry (SFPA)

1985	For Spacers Snarled in the Hair of Comets
1987	The Nightmare Collector
1994	Spacer's Compass
1995	Future Present: A Lesson in Expectation
2001	My Wife Returns as She Would Have It

Balticon Poetry Award

2005	Why Your Robot Dog Has Been Recalcitrant
2010	The Veracity of Imagination
2013	The Music of the Stars

Boomerang Award (Aboriginal SF Readers Award)

1988	Against the Ebon Rush of Night

SFPA Poetry Contest (Dwarf Form Category)

2014	Surreal Shopping List

Acknowledgments

For advice in compiling this collection, my thanks go to Marge Simon, and also to my friends on Facebook, whose "likes" and comments helped me decide what poems to include in *Artifacts*.

Omissions

Short poems not considered for this collection include prose poems, collaborations, and solo poems from *Chronicles of the Mutant Rain*, *Notes from the Shadow City*, and *Sacrificial Nights*. These can be found in the following collections:

Short Circuits (Ocean View Books, 1991)
Chronicles of the Mutant Rain Forest (with Robert Frazier, Horror's Head Press, 1992)
Flashing the Dark (Sam's Dot Publishing, 2006)
Double Visions (collaborative poems, Dark Regions Press, 2009)
Notes from the Shadow City (with Gary William Crawford, Dark Regions Press, 2012)
Sacrificial Nights (with Alessandro Manzetti, Kipple Officina Libraria, 2016)

Bruce Boston is the author of more than fifty books and chapbooks, including the dystopian science fiction novel *The Guarderer's Tale*. His writing has appeared in hundreds of publications, including *Analog, Asimov's SF Magazine, Amazing Stories, Realms of Fantasy, Strange Horizons, Weird Tales, The Pedestal Magazine, Daily Science Fiction, Year's Best Fantasy and Horror*, and *The Nebula Awards Showcase*. Considered one of the leading genre poets for more than thirty years, his poetry has received numerous awards, including the Bram Stoker Award, the *Asimov's* Readers Award, the Rhysling Award, the Balticon Poetry Award, the Gothic Readers Choice Award, and the Grandmaster Award of the Science Fiction Poetry Association. His fiction has received a Pushcart Prize and twice been a Bram Stoker Award Finalist (novel, short story). He lives in Ocala, Florida with his wife, writer-artist Marge Simon. www.bruceboston.com.

Luke Spooner currently lives and works in the South of England. Having graduated from the University of Portsmouth with a first-class degree he is now a fulltime illustrator working under two aliases: "Carrion House" for his darker work and "Hoodwink House" for his work aimed at a younger audience. He believes that the job of putting someone else's words into a visual form, to accompany and support their text, is a massive responsibility as well as being something he truly treasures.

If you enjoyed this book, I'm sure you'll also like the following Crystal Lake titles:

Gutted: Beautiful Horror Stories
http://getbook.at/Gutted

An anthology of dark fiction that explores the beauty at the very heart of darkness. Featuring horror's most celebrated voices: Clive Barker, Neil Gaiman, Ramsey Campbell, Paul Tremblay, John F.D. Taff, Lisa Mannetti, Damien Angelica Walters, Josh Malerman, Christopher Coake, Mercedes M. Yardley, Brian Kirk, Stephanie M. Wytovich, Amanda Gowin, Richard Thomas, Maria Alexander, and Kevin Lucia.

Eden Underground
http://getbook.at/AmazonEden

Horror poetry by Alessandro Manzetti – Another snake, another tree, another Eve. A surreal journey into obsessions and aberrations of the modern world and the darker side, which often takes control of the situation. Winner of the 2014 Bram Stoker Award for Superior Achievement in Poetry.

Or check out other Crystal Lake Publishing titles for your Dark Fiction, Horror, Suspense, and Thriller needs.

www.crystallakepub.com/books

We hope you enjoyed this title. If so, we'd be grateful if you could leave a review on your blog or any of the other websites and outlets open to book reviews. Reviews are like gold to writers and publishers, since word-of-mouth is and will always be the best way to market a great book. And remember to keep an eye out for more of our books.

Connect with Crystal Lake Publishing

Website:
www.crystallakepub.com
Be sure to sign up for our newsletter and receive
a free eBook: http://eepurl.com/xfuKP

Facebook:
www.facebook.com/Crystallakepublishing

Twitter:
https://twitter.com/crystallakepub

Blog:
http://www.crystallakepub.com/blog-2/

Instagram:
https://www.instagram.com/crystal_lake_publishing/

Patreon:
https://www.patreon.com/CLP

YouTube:
https://www.youtube.com/c/CrystalLakePublishing

With unmatched success since 2012, Crystal Lake Publishing has quickly become one of the world's leading indie publishers of Mystery, Thriller, and Suspense books with a Dark Fiction edge.

Crystal Lake Publishing puts integrity, honor and respect at the forefront of our operations.

We strive for each book and outreach program that's launched to not only entertain and touch or comment on issues that affect our readers, but also to strengthen and support the Dark Fiction field and its authors.

Not only do we publish authors who are legends in the field and as hardworking as us, but we look for men and women who care about their readers and fellow human beings. We only publish the very best Dark Fiction, and look forward to launching many new careers.

We strive to know each and every one of our readers, while building personal relationships with our authors, reviewers, bloggers, pod-casters, bookstores and libraries.

Crystal Lake Publishing is and will always be a beacon of what passion and dedication, combined with overwhelming teamwork and respect, can accomplish: Unique fiction you can't find anywhere else.

We do not just publish books, we present you worlds within your world, doors within your mind, from talented authors who sacrifice so much for a moment of your time.

This is what we believe in. What we stand for. This will be our legacy.

Welcome to Crystal Lake Publishing.

THANK YOU FOR PURCHASING THIS eBOOK

www.ingramcontent.com/pod-product-compliance
Lightning Source LLC
Chambersburg PA
CBRC091725070526
44586CB00007B/80